Quiz # 2592

RL 4.3

Pts . 0.5

Read All About

CATS

MAINE COON CATS

LYNN M. STONE

The Rourke Corporation, Inc.
Vero Beach, Florida 32964

PHOTO CREDITS
All photos © Lynn M. Stone

ACKNOWLEDGEMENTS
The author thanks Sandy Doherty of Johns Bay Maine Coons (Barrington,
IL) for her assistance—and her cats—in the preparation of this book.

CREATIVE SERVICES:
East Coast Studios, Merritt Island, Florida

EDITORIAL SERVICES:
Janice L. Smith for Penworthy Learning Systems

Library of Congress Cataloging-in-Publication Data

Stone, Lynn M.
  Maine coon cats / by Lynn M. Stone.
    p. cm. — (Cats)
  Includes bibliographical references (p. 24) and index.
  Summary: Provides an introduction to the history, physical
characteristics, and breeding of Maine coon cats.
    ISBN 0-86593-553-X
  1. Maine coon cat Juvenile literature. [1. Maine coon cat. 2. Cats.] I.
Title. II. Series: Stone, Lynn M.- Cats.
SF449.M34S76 1999
636.8'3—dc21
                                           99-27277
                                             CIP

Printed in the USA

TABLE OF CONTENTS

Maine Coon Cats 5

Cat Breeds 8

What a Maine Coon Cat Looks Like . .12

The History of Maine Coon Cats 17

Owning a Maine Coon 20

Glossary 23

Index 24

Further Reading 24

MAINE COON CATS

Some people think that the Maine coon cat does, indeed, have a raccoon or two among its **ancestors** (AN SESS terz). After all, the long-haired Maine coon cat loves to climb trees. And the first Maine coon cats had dark rings of color in their bushy tails. Despite its name, though, the Maine coon cat is not part raccoon.

The long hairs at the tips of a Maine coon cat's ears are tufts. Not all Maine coons have them.

The Maine coon cat is all cat. It's a big, tough cat, too, and a fine hunter. With its ear tufts, a Maine coon more closely resembles its wild cousin the **lynx** (LYNGKS) than a raccoon. Could the Maine coon, then, be part lynx? No, but somewhere in its background, long ago, was a wild cat.

Maine coon cats love to prowl outdoors. This cat carries its bushy tail like a flag.

A silvery Maine coon stares with round, golden eyes. Cats see well in low light, but they don't see in sharp focus or in full color.

That wild ancestor was the little wildcat of Africa and Asia. Nearly all **domestic** (duh MESS tik), or tame, cats share this relative.

Maine coons are one of several **breeds** (BREEDZ), or kinds, of long-haired cats. They are similar to the Siberian and Norwegian forest cats.

CAT BREEDS

Purebred (PEUR BRED) cats are those which belong to a certain breed, like Maine coons. A breed of cats, or a breed of any animal, comes about with the help of people.

All cats are basically the same animal. But people who raised cats, cat breeders, began to favor certain cats a long time ago. They recognized that not all the kittens in a house cat's **litter** (LIT er) were exactly alike.

Breeds of cats are usually separated by features other than color. This Persian's face and body build, rather than fur color, separate it from other long-haired cats, like the Maine coon.

Breeders chose certain cats for their size, shape, color, or behavior. By using those handpicked cats as the mothers and fathers for future litters, breeders got kittens that were much like their parents.

Over many hundreds of years, breeders developed groups of cats. Each group had something special about it, like its color, shape, length of fur, or even its voice. In time, these groups became what we call breeds. Today there are about 80 breeds of cats.

The Maine coon was one of the first truly American breeds. There have been many breeds since the Maine coon, and there will be even more.

The Maine coon's handsome looks and easygoing personality have made it a popular cat worldwide.

WHAT A MAINE COON CAT LOOKS LIKE

The Maine coon looks its best in winter. Then its coat is thick and shiny.

A Maine coon cat's coat can be any of several different colors. The first Maine coons were generally brown with darker stripes and white trim. That color pattern is still popular.

The first Maine coons looked like long-haired tiger cats.

Large, upright ears, a square muzzle, a long, bushy tail, and glossy fur help distinguish the Maine coon from other breeds.

Another popular color is a reddish-orange with tabby striping. Some Maine coons are solid colors, such as black, cream, or white. In England, Maine coon cat breeders have listed at least 64 color patterns for their cats.

The color of a Maine coon isn't what sets it apart from other breeds. A cat's fur, body size, and other features help identify it as a Maine coon.

Maine coon cats, for instance, have long fur with a special feel to it. They have round eyes, large ears (often with tufts), and a tail that would make a fox proud!

Maine coons also have big bodies. Maine coons may weigh up to 22 pounds (10 kilograms). A big male Maine coon—a tomcat, as male cats are known—isn't much lighter than a female **bobcat** (BAHB KAT)!

Purebred Maine coons usually have green, gold, or orange eyes. White Maine coons, however, may have blue eyes or "odd eyes." Each eye is a different color in odd-eyed cats.

The ear tufts of the wild lynx give it a look similar to the Maine coon cat.

THE HISTORY OF MAINE COON CATS

The history of the Maine coon cats is like that of most of the older cat breeds. It's not very clear. It is likely, however, that the Maine coon's ancestors arrived in Maine at seaports. Ships from Europe, arriving in Maine, often had cats aboard. Some of them, no doubt, slipped ashore. They must have decided that life in the Maine woods was better than life at sea.

Some of those European cats were probably longhairs from Russia and Scandinavia. They were most likely the ancestors of the first cats called Maine coons. In 1861 a black-and-white Maine coon, named Captain Jenks, was shown in Boston and New York.

Captain Jenks, the first Maine coon to be shown, was black and white. Black-and-white Maine coons are not very common today.

People liked Captain Jenks and the other Maine coons that followed. The big, shaggy cats became quite popular.

Around 1900, however, Persian cats became the favorite of long-haired cat lovers. The Maine coon lasted as a breed largely because of farmers. Farmers liked the cats because they were all-star rat and mouse catchers!

Interest in the Maine coon was renewed in the 1950s. Today the breed enjoys great popularity.

Alert to every movement and sound, a Maine coon cat is a fine hunter. Cats are nature's most nearly perfect predators.

Much greater interest in Maine coons returned in the 1950s. That interest has continued. Today Maine coons and Himalayans are the two most popular cat breeds in the United States.

OWNING A MAINE COON

Maine coon cats are sometimes described as buddies rather than babies. They're hardy cats, so they can take care of themselves.

Maine coons like people, and they often greet their human companions with a happy chirp. Maine coons like a warm lap now and then, but they don't need human baby-sitters.

Maine coons are fairly independent. They seem quite content to find their own activities. Sometimes their activities include a swim!

A female Maine coon perches on an end table. The cat's long outer coat hides an undercoat of fur.

GLOSSARY

ancestor (AN SESS ter) — those in the past from whom a person or animal has descended

bobcat (BAHB KAT) — a medium-sized wild cat with a stubby (bobbed) tail

breed (BREED) — a particular group of domestic animals having several of the same characteristics; a kind of domestic animal within a group of many kinds, such as a *Bengal* cat or a *Persian* cat

domestic (duh MESS tik) — a type of animal that has been tamed and raised by humans for hundreds of years

litter (LIT er) — a group of kittens born at a single time

lynx (LINGKS) — a medium-sized wild cat with long legs and ear tufts

purebred (PEUR BRED) — a domestic animal of a single (pure) breed

Every cat, even home-raised purebreds, will still be "hobby hunters" if given the chance. Maine coons survived as a breed largely because farmers liked their hunting skills.

INDEX

bobcat   14

breeders   8, 11

breeds   8, 11, 13, 17

cats   8, 11

   domestic   7

   Himalayan   19

   Maine coon   5, 6, 7, 8, 11, 12, 13, 14, 17, 18, 19, 20

   Norwegian forest   7

   Persian   18

   purebred   8

   Siberian forest   7

wild   6

coat   12

colors   11, 13

ear tufts   6, 14

farmers   18

fur   13, 14

kittens   11

litters   8, 11

lynx   6

Maine   17

raccoon   5

tails   5, 14

FURTHER READING

Find out more about Maine Coon cats and cats in general with these helpful books and information sites:

- Clutton-Brock, Juliet. *Cat.* Knopf, 1997
- Editors of Owl Magazine. *The Kids' Cat Book.* Greey de Pencier, 1990
- Evans, Mark. *ASPCA Pet Care Guide for Kids/Kittens.* Dorling Kindersley, 1992
- Scott, Carey. *Kittens.* Dorling Kindersley, 1992
- Maine Coon Breeders and Fanciers Association, 4405 Karrol S.W., Albuquerque, NM 87121
- Cat Fanciers' Association on line @ www.cfainc.org